MW01016319

You're off to a
great start!

How To Fly

Relaxed & Happy
From Takeoff To Touchdown

By Natalie Windsor
Illustrations by Joe Azar

CorkScrew Press
Los Angeles

Distribution in U.S.: PDS, 6893 Sullivan Road, Grawn, MI 49637
In Canada: Firefly Books, Ltd., 250 Sparks Ave., Willowdale, Ontario M2H 2S4

Library of Congress Cataloging-in-Publication Data
Windsor, Natalie.
     How To Fly : relaxed & happy from takeoff to touchdown / by
Natalie Windsor : illustrations by Joe Azar.

     1. Air travel.   2. Air travel—Psychological aspects.
3. Aeronautics, Commercial—Passenger traffic.   I. Azar, Joe.
II. Title.
HE9787.W56   1993   387.7'42'019—dc20   93-12139
ISBN 0-944042-25-2

Single-copy orders: see page 158. For quantity discounts and imprintings for sales promotions, premiums, fund-raising and educational uses, please write to the Publisher.

Manufactured in the U.S.A.

10   9   8   7   6   5   4   3   2   1

"Time is the longest distance between two places."

—*Tennessee Williams*

To Arthur, Rich & Joe.
With love, gratitude and admiration.

Acknowledgements

Many thanks to the people who lent their knowledge and wisdom to this book: Charles N. Barnard, travel editor, *Modern Maturity;* Lisa Beezley; Jill Bradley, PT; Barry Brayer, FAA; Elly Brekke, FAA; Herb Chapin; Joel Chineson; Chris English; Ann George; Bill Hoffer, National Weather Service; Agnes J. Huff, Ph.D.; Pat Jorgenson, U.S. Geological Survey; Lionel Kauffler; Timothy Kelly, U.S. Department of Transportation; Arthur Lampel, JD; Bob Matthews, manager of safety promotion, FAA; David Melancon, Association of Flight Attendants; Ilan Migdali, L. Ac; Prof. Peter Monkewitz, UCLA Department of Mechanical & Aerospace Engineering; Dr. Robert Murphy, DDS; Mike & Helen O'Brien; Jon A. Pace, hypnotherapist; Donna Panullo; Jerry, Rebecca & the entire PDS crew; Fred Pelzman, Community & Consumer Liaison Division, FAA; Wendy Perrin, ombudsman editor, *Condé Nast Traveler;* Emily Porter, public relations, ASTA; Patti Putnicki; Ro & Shel; Peter Shaw-Lawrence, Society for the Advancement of Travel for the Handicapped; Steve Spar; Patrick Walsh, American Airlines Flight Service Manager and fellow flight attendants at DFW; Cara & Tim Walter; Arnie Willcuts, SMOKENDERS; and the many flight attendants, reservation agents, frequent flyers and nervous passengers interviewed for this book. May all your flights be comfortable, safe and on time.

Design by Ken Niles, *Ad Infinitum*

In theory, flying is wonderful. We soar safely above the clouds, see places we might only read about, and visit loved ones across the country as easily as if they lived across town.

In practice, flying is something else. We stand around, drag bags, tense up, sit cramped, and arrive tired.

After years of flying and talking with all kinds of passengers, I've discovered one thing that brings the practice closer to the theory. *The secret is to know what's going on around you.* I hope this book will make your experience inspiring, easier and most of all, fun.

So, if you're traveling on business — close a big deal. On vacation — go for the gusto. Visiting family — hug someone special.

Natalie Windsor
118° 14′ 28″ west / 34° 3′ 15″ north

Welcome Aboard!

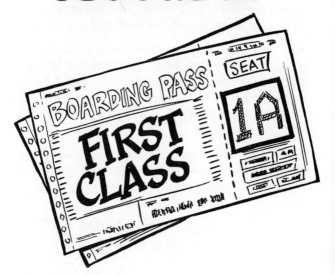

**Your instant check-in
to *How to Fly* highlights**

Complete contents next page ➜

To Prepare You

Page 142

To Inform You

To Calm You

Page 146

Page 30

To Protect You

To Relax You

To Challenge You

To Entertain You

Page 35

How lucky we are to have such freedom of travel!

150 years ago people packed their lives into covered wagons and spent months riding over rugged trails, constantly facing danger, hardship and disease.

100 years ago people loaded their lives into steamer trunks deep in the holds of crowded ships. The long weeks at sea meant many would never go back to their old homes again.

50 years ago air travel was available only to the very rich and the very brave. Early propeller planes bounced adventurers across unfriendly skies.

Today we can kiss loved ones goodbye in the morning — visit faraway cities — and return home in time to kiss them goodnight. Air travel gives us control over our time and our world.

We are truly lucky to be able to fly.

NOW PLAYING!

Welcome to the best seats in the house — a real Sky Box — where you can observe the glory of nature from a vantage point few others in history were ever privileged to have. Here we go . . . the show is about to begin!

The
AMAZING
REAL-LIFE
NATURE
MOVING
Picture
Show

& PHYSICS CARTOON

The Clouds Below

One of the most exhilarating experiences is to take off on a dark, rainy day and within a few minutes be flying through bright sunshine and blue skies. Soaring above the clouds gives you the thrill of watching the weather at work, safely, like no TV newscaster can show you. Clouds are giant clues to the weather . . . if you know how to read them.

Essentially, clouds are nothing more than tiny ice crystals and fine water droplets. They're formed by movements of air and by changes in temperature and altitude. We can't see through them, but a pilot's instruments can.

Clouds come in all shapes and sizes, but actually fall into categories which make them easy to identify.

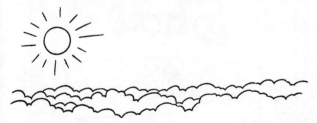

Cirrus

Cirrus clouds are highest, appearing as feathery white streaks in the cold air above 20,000 feet. They're made entirely of ice crystals carried along by winds of varying speeds. When a faster wind picks up the main part of the cloud, some of the remaining ice crystals trail behind, forming what are commonly called "mares' tails."

Stratus

Stratus clouds form in layers or sheets and are made of tiny water droplets. From the ground, you see stratus clouds as a familiar low-hanging gray ceiling, often accompanied by fog or drizzle. As your plane climbs, you may also see stratus clouds at higher levels, called altostratus and cirrostratus, indicating stable air masses. Above these clouds, you'll only get rare glimpses of the ground; but don't worry, it's still there.

Cumulus

Cumulus clouds are big, white and fluffy. Joni Mitchell celebrated them as "ice-cream castles in the air." They occur in rising warm air; in small groups they indicate fair weather. If you're flying over the ocean in a clear blue sky, look for small puffs in the distance. It probably means there are islands below them.

Cumulus clouds can grow to dramatic proportions several thousand feet high and are beautiful to behold. You usually see them from the side because pilots will fly around them.

Why Is The Sky Blue?

It depends who's asking.

If it's YOU, here's the scoop: Sunlight is actually a combination of all colors of the spectrum, each one traveling on a different wavelength. When light hits the earth's atmosphere, the invisible air molecules scatter only the shorter blue and violet rays, and let the others pass through. This infinite scattering fills the sky with continuous blue light.

When skies are gray, it's because larger particles in the air are scattering more wavelengths from the spectrum. Water droplets in clouds scatter all wavelengths, making the clouds appear white. Pollution particles are the right size to create yellow or brownish colors. Sunsets are fiery red because only the longer red and orange wavelengths can escape through the dense lower atmosphere to light up the sky.

And if it's your KID who's asking, the answer is, "Just because."

Free Light Shows

Flying high above the weather gives you a clear advantage over ground-bound folks to see a few of nature's spectacular light phenomena.

Round rainbows

At ground-level, your view is limited, so you can only see the part of a rainbow that arcs to somewhere over the horizon. But from the air, you can see the entire rainbow in its dazzling full-circle display!

Glowing glories

As you fly above layers of clouds, try to spot the plane's shadow on them. If conditions are right, you'll witness a "glory" — a circle of colored light around the shadow. Sometimes you'll see only the glory, if the plane is too high to cast a shadow. You're not likely to see a glory at ground level, but watch for them from your window seat.

Clues In The Landscape

The changing scenery on the ground is part science, part modern art and part poetry — a testament to both natural forces and human ingenuity. And just like a walk through a museum, if you don't know what you're looking at, you'll miss the richness of the experience.

For starters, look in the back of your in-flight magazine for the airline route map and trace your own flight path. A good map will show topographical features, like the mountains and plains you'll cross.

You can tell the relative ages of mountains by their features. High mountains with sharp, jagged edges are the youngsters — from 70 to 250 million years old — the tough erosion forces of wind, water and ice haven't worn them down. When you're crossing the western two-thirds of the U.S., study the Rockies and the Sierra Nevada.

You want old? Check out the Appalachians, stretching from Maine to Alabama. See how

600 million years of erosion have turned the Berkshires, Adirondacks and Blue Ridge Mountains into soft, rounded, tree-covered humps.

Many rivers show up as long silver ribbons threading through the landscape. You may first spot the tell-tale clumps of trees that line most river banks before you even catch a glimpse of a river. Follow them to see where the river runs.

You can tell if a river is old and lazy by looking for large loops in its course, like the Mississippi River below St. Louis. A younger river, like the Columbia between Washington and Oregon, tends to run straight.

The human footprint

The vast checkerboard of the Great Plains and Midwest was created by ownership boundaries and various farming methods. In the semi-arid climate of Kansas and Nebraska, bright green circles watered by center-pivot irrigation systems stand out in a brown and golden quilt. And here, rows of trees separating fields do not indicate river banks; rather they shield loose soil from relentless winds.

Leaving the Midwest, look for the crooked and seemingly haphazard patchwork of land east of the

Mississippi River. This reflects the Old World system of property division, where each parcel of land was allowed to border at least part of a stream.

Roads also provide clues to the terrain. Straight lines indicate level ground, while twists and turns follow the contours of land with varying elevations.

Cities located on coastlines and major waterways give away their old age. More recent cities developed inland as rail and highway hubs, reflecting the nation's rich transportation history.

Why Planes Fly 101

If we learned the secrets of flight from the birds, then how on earth does a plane get off the ground without flapping its wings?

Early inventors kept trying to copy the only model of flying they knew — and kept falling flat — until they discovered that two forces are involved in flying, lift and thrust, and were able to harness each force separately.

Lift

You've already experienced lift first-hand when you've put your arm outside the window of a moving car. By holding your fingers together pointed into the wind, and tilting your palm up slightly, you felt an upward pull created by suction along the back of your hand. That's lift. Amazingly, you can get the same result by simply arching your palm. And if you try both tilting and arching together, you'll understand how the shape of a wing lifts the plane. (Try this at home, not on the plane!) Actual lift is determined by the wing's size, angle of tilt and

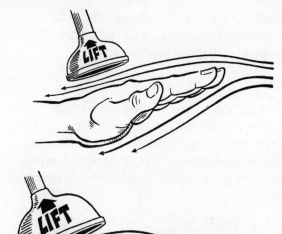

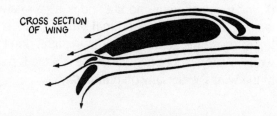

CROSS SECTION
OF WING

the speed of the plane. And any object can be carried in the air, regardless of size or weight, if it's equipped with the right-sized wings.

Thrust

While lift acts to counter the plane's weight, thrust is the forward propulsion needed to overcome the "drag" caused by the plane's resistance to the air. In birds, thrust comes from flapping their wings; in planes, it's produced by power from propellers or jet engines.

Controlling flight

The key to smooth flying is controlling thrust and lift together. Pilots do this by adjusting the flaps, slats and spoilers on the wings during take-off, landing and for steering. The best seats for seeing these carefully orchestrated movements are from the rear third of the plane.

Wings are also designed to flex up and down during flight, offering smoother rides. It's a safety feature, and it's perfectly normal. And if you see liquid streaming across the wings in flight, don't worry. Water vapor often condenses on the top side of the wings, especially on humid days.

WINGS THAT FLY

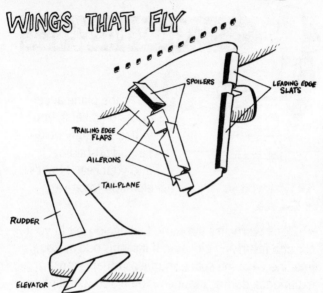

SPOILERS

LEADING EDGE SLATS

TRAILING EDGE FLAPS

AILERONS

TAILPLANE

RUDDER

ELEVATOR

WINGS THAT DON'T

WING TIP

WATER WINGS

BUFFALO WINGS

WINGBACK

Gee!-Force

As the plane accelerates on takeoff, you will feel slightly heavier and pushed back into your seat. No, it's not what you ate. It's the acceleration force — or G-force.

Don't worry. It's the same feeling you get in your car or a fast-rising elevator. If it seems odd to you, imagine what the space shuttle astronauts must experience during a launch. You'll also feel slightly more G-force when the pilot changes direction on banked turns.

No astronaut experience would be complete without weightlessness, and at some point during the flight — as the plane quickly levels off right after takeoff, or on descent — you may suddenly feel a little lighter in your seat. It's that fast-moving elevator again, this time going back to the lobby. Enjoy it. You'll never lose weight more easily.

Headwinds Or Tailwinds?

If you've ever headed into a strong wind with an open umbrella, you can appreciate the job the plane has to do. Every ten miles-per-hour of headwind adds ten miles to the distance the plane must fly every hour. On the other hand, tailwinds go in the same direction as the plane, helping to carry it along faster and save fuel. The airlines build these factors into their schedules.

Turbulence is simply air that isn't smooth. It usually feels like riding over a bumpy street in a bus. Pilots can tell where turbulence occurs and try to steer clear of it. If they do go through it, stay calm. They'll tell you to fasten your seatbelt while they head toward smoother air.

Hisssssssssssssss

Name That Noise

The Normal Sounds of Air Travel

Clomp! Thunk! Whir-r-r! What the heck was that? Don't worry. Those are just some of the harmless noises you hear on takeoff, landing and occasionally during flight. Here's what causes some of them:

➤ Luggage being loaded into the belly of the plane *whumps* and *thuds* beneath the floor.

➤ Air conditioning units may also vibrate and *hummm* under your feet.

➤ The covered ramp connecting the terminal to the plane *whirrs* away from the door.

➤ New brake pads can *grind* during taxiing or landing.

CLUNK!

flick

➤ Landing wheels *clomp* as they lock into position, and *thunk* when retracted back into their housings. You may also hear the housing doors *clank* shut.

WHOOOOOSH

➤ The angles of the wing flaps and slats are deliberately adjusted during takeoffs and landings. You may hear them *flick* or *whirr* into place.

flick flick CLOMP!

➤ The air nozzle over your seat may *hiss.* If it bugs you, reach up and screw it shut.

➤ Normal landings include *thumps, screeches* from the wheels, *whines* from the flaps, and a long *loud roar* as the engines are set to slow the plane down.

Hisssssssssssss

If This Is Your
First
Flight

(or even
if it isn't.)

Here's a quick overview of the essentials for
smooth traveling. Most items are more thoroughly
covered in the pages that follow. And don't forget to
review the Last-Minute Flight Check on page 122.

Before leaving for the airport

➤ Always call the airline to re-confirm your flight and ask about any delays.

➤ Memorize your flight number, departure time, airline's name and any connecting flight information.

➤ Make sure your ticket, passport, personal IDs and luggage keys are secure but quickly accessible.

➤ Double-check your luggage and carry-on bags — are they properly labeled? See page 52.

➤ Check the weather forecast for your destination. Pack last minute items accordingly.

➤ Make a list of everything you pack, and carry it with you. You'll need it for insurance reimbursement if your luggage never arrives.

➤ Keep plenty of small bills handy for curbside tipping.

➤ Plan to arrive at the airport at least one hour before departure — earlier during peak periods — and at least two hours ahead for an international flight.

On arriving at the airport

➤If possible, check your bags at curbside and
  avoid long lines at the ticket counters. The convenience is well worth the extra dollar or two
  per bag for the tip.

➤Check the closest departure monitor for your
  gate number and any schedule changes. Make
  sure you're *at the gate* at least 30 minutes before
  flight time for domestic flights and one hour for
  international flights.

➤Every airport announcement may affect you —
  don't tune them out. You can even hear them in
  the restrooms and eateries.

➤Some airports offer inter-denominational
  chapels, if you would be more comfortable
  checking in with you-know-Who before you fly.

➤Always keep close watch on your carry-on bags
  and personal belongings, especially as you go
  through the metal detector. See page 49.

Before you board

➤ When you arrive at the gate, check in with the agent — even if you already have a seat assignment.

➤ Don't wander too far from the gate area — you may miss the boarding announcement. However, if you have time, make an "insurance" trip to the restroom.

➤ The safest place for purses, briefcases or carry-on bags is between your feet, whether you're standing in line or sitting in the gate area.

➤ If you try to carry on an oversized item — like a garment bag or musical instrument — the attendants may insist you check it at the gate. By flying at non-peak times, there may be room on board to make exceptions.

➤ If you plan on taking motion medication, do it now so it's in full effect during your flight.

➤ If your flight is delayed, overbooked or cancelled, see pages 62–65.

On the plane

➤ Before you settle in, make sure your seat is the one listed on your boarding pass.

➤ If you are seated in an emergency exit row, and don't want the extra responsibilities, request a different seat.

➤ As quickly as possible, put your carry-on items in the closest available overhead bin or completely under the seat in front of you. If you need help, ask.

➤ Pay attention to the safety announcement and memorize the way to all the emergency exits.

➤ If you feel a draft — or if you're too warm — you can adjust the airflow nozzle over your head. Cabin temperature will stabilize once you're airborne. If you remain uncomfortable, tell the flight attendant.

➤ Your access to the lavatory may be restricted during flight, or blocked by the cart during beverage and meal service. Plan your trips accordingly.

➤ Boy, were you smart to bring something to read!

Upon landing

➤ Be extra careful opening the overhead bin. Things shift during flight, and could tumble onto your head.

➤ Pay attention to all announcements, and stay seated with your seatbelt fastened until the sign is turned off.

➤ Set your watch to local time.

➤ Check your entire seating area to ensure you have all of your belongings.

Captain Wrightway's Guide To Proper Cabin Etiquette.

- Adjust your seatback gently, or the person behind you might suddenly be wearing hot coffee.

- Replace your tray table slowly, or the person in front of you may have a rude awakening.

- In daylight hours, keep your window shade closed during a movie, or when everyone else on the plane is asleep.

- If you're a frequent lavatory-user, book an aisle seat. Or trade with the person next to you.

- Keep in-flight necessities under the seat in front of you. Constant trips to the overhead bin agitate seatmates.

- Talk softly on the airphone. No one really wants to hear the details of Aunt Edna's operation.

- Hand your trash to the flight attendant when they come asking for it. Don't find clever new places to hide it.

- Always listen to the flight attendants. There are important safety reasons for their requests.

- At the end of your flight, wait for the announcement before removing your seatbelt and opening overhead bins.

Your Best Friend In Travel Is Free

Top-notch travel agents are worth their weight in chocolate and emeralds. They do all the work, save you money, book your plane, car and hotel — and they don't cost you anything. Plus, if your plans suddenly change, you have a guardian angel at home plugged into all the right networks. Find a good one the same way you found your dentist:

➤ Check with friends, colleagues and relatives. Who saved them money? Time? Hassles?

➤ Does the agency have a toll-free number? Are they members of the American Society of Travel Agents? Is there a Certified Travel Counselor on staff?

➤ Ask if they offer a computerized low-fare-check system to hunt for bargains and fare reductions.

➤ Do they cater to your particular needs, such as group tours, cruises, business travel or traveling with a disability?

Get The Lowest Airfare

You may have paid a different fare than the guy sitting next to you. Here's how to make sure yours is lower:

➤ When you make your reservations, tell your travel agent or airline ticket agent that you want the least expensive fare — don't assume they know.

➤ Purchase your ticket well in advance. In most cases, the closer to your departure date, the higher your ticket price.

➤ Be flexible. You can save lots of money by flying at the airline's convenience.

➤ Airfare wars often occur suddenly. Watch newspaper ads for short-term discount fares *and call immediately.* Be prepared to pay within 24 hours or lose your reservation. You can also call other airlines to see if they'll match the lower fare.

➤ Keep tabs on airfares *after* you purchase your ticket. If the fare goes down, some airlines will credit you with the difference — but only if you ask.

When Booking A Flight

This is the time to say what you want, ask lots of questions, nail down the details and avoid that "Darn, I shoulda checked" feeling.

➤It's fine to make reservations by phone, but tickets aren't issued until you pay for them. Airlines and travel agents will accept most credit cards, and will mail your tickets to you.

➤Paying by credit card can also offer some hidden advantages — like automatic travel insurance and extra luggage and carry-on bag insurance. Check with your credit card company. Plus, if your airline goes bankrupt, you can refuse to pay for your unused ticket.

➤Ask about restrictions on your ticket, like non-refundability, penalties for changes, etc. If they give you a code number, write it down, and mention it when you call back. Be sure to give them your frequent flyer number, too.

➤Specify the seat you want, and ask for your boarding pass now, to save time at the gate. See page 44 for best seat selection.

➤Special meals are available only if you request them in advance, including vegetarian, low-sodium, low-cholesterol, low-calorie, gluten-free, kosher, Moslem, diabetic or children's meals.

➤When you get your ticket, check to make sure all the information is accurate — including your name. Have any corrections made immediately.

➤Ask about restrictions on the size, weight and number of bags you can bring on all flights: domestic, international and connecting. Will there be any hidden charges abroad, such as customs fees or departure taxes?

➤The airline automatically insures your bags, but the amount can vary and may not fully cover your valuables. Ask about "excess valuation insurance," which must be purchased at the airport.

Smart Seating

Many people don't state a seat preference — or just accept what they're given — but your overall comfort and convenience during the trip can depend on where you sit.

Aisle seats

➤ Good for quick exits, access to overhead luggage bin and easy trips to the lavatory.

➤ Bad for overhanging elbows and trying to sleep, especially when your seatmate needs to go to the restroom. Again and again.

Window seats

➤ Great for sight-seeing, sleeping and head support (with a pillow). If you want a good view, avoid sitting over the wing; but you'll get the smoothest ride there.

➤ To avoid the harsh sunlight on north-south routes, reserve seats accordingly. For example, on a southbound flight in the morning, sit on the right-hand side of the plane.

Middle seats

➤ The only advantage is they allow you to sit next to your companion. It's smarter to book the aisle and window seats together — and switch on board if the middle seat gets assigned to a third person.

Front vs. back

➤ Rows close to the front offer a smoother, quieter ride, but may be more crowded and packed with kids. You'll be last on, but first off. Ideal for tight connections.

➤ Rows in the back may have more engine noise, but tend to be less crowded. You'll be closer to the lavatories and service galleys — but if possible, avoid sitting right next to them.

All dialogue guaranteed spoken to airline reservation agents.

✈ Man calls airline's 800-number from pay phone at airport, looks over at ticket counter and asks, "Which one of you am I talking to? Raise your hand."

✈ Woman is told she'll have to make one change between Newark and Los Angeles. Demands to know why she'll need to change clothes.

✈ Caller says, "My kitchen" when asked where she's calling from.

✈ Man asks if his flight stops at Exit 7A on the New Jersey Turnpike.

✈ Someone calls to say the flight was "bumpy and the peanuts were stale."

✈ Caller wants a morning flight that leaves "around 7 p.m."

✈ Caller says, "Today is the 19th. If I leave tomorrow, what day will that be?"

✈ After agent confirms lengthy reservation and repeats all flight information, caller says, "Maybe I should write this down."

Be Too Smart
To Be Scammed.

irports are full of busy rushing people loaded with luggage, cash and valuables — making them ideal targets for professional thieves and con artists. Here are a few well-tested scams aimed at unsuspecting passengers, which rake in several hundred million dollars each year. Don't fall prey to their scams.

The Pass-Through Interception

Some overzealous metal detectors will beep at any metallic objects in your pockets. While you're emptying your pockets and doing the terminal two-step, your unattended belongings are ripe for plucking at the other end by anyone who acts like the owner. It takes only a second.

Your best defense: Watch your things at all times. If you're traveling with a companion, take turns guarding your things as you go through one at a time.

The Distract-&-Grab Scam

Beware of the helpful stranger who points out the fresh splotch of ketchup or other stain on your clothing. Guess how it got there. He or she may be setting you up for a classic "distract-and- grab" scam, usually with several accomplices. While your attention is diverted, someone else makes off with your unwatched items. Variations of this ruse are endless: a couple suddenly starts an argument right next to you; a stranger asks for directions or change, or speaks to you in a foreign language.

Your best defense: Whenever a stranger approaches you, or you see a suspicious distraction, rely on your sixth sense. It could be nothing, or the beginning of a ruined trip. Keep your things close to you, never take your eyes — or hands — off them. *Any* confusion or distraction is your cue to instantly double your guard.

The Phone Card Scam

Eagle-eyed thieves with binoculars memorize your long-distance phone card number by watching you tap it in at pay phones. You could find hundreds of dollars in calls on your phone bill to places you've never even heard of.

Your best defense: Memorize your number, or don't hold up your card as you dial. Shield your fingers and stand close to the phone. If you're traveling internationally, inform your long-distance company in advance so their computer won't shut off your service when it detects unusual calling patterns on your card.

C.Y.T.
(Cover Your Tushie)

➤ Write down the serial numbers of your travelers checks together with the phone number to call for replacements. Always keep this separate from the checks.

➤ Carry travelers checks separate from your passport and other ID. Stolen checks may be passed without question when backed up by another form of ID.

➤ If you carry a checkbook, insert a new register pad before leaving home. Why reveal your hefty bank balance to prying eyes every time you write a check?

➤ Security wallets and money belts come in all shapes and sizes to fit you comfortably. Wear one — send pickpockets away empty-handed.

➤ If you carry cash in big wads, it can be legally confiscated in airports by the Drug Enforcement Administration if they suspect you of drug-related activity. Even if you're released after questioning, the DEA can hold money as evidence — and you'll have to sue to get it back. See the list of property seizures Wednesdays in *USA Today*.

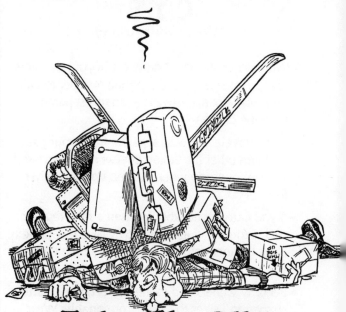

Take The Lug Out Of Luggage.

Packing your bags doesn't have to be a drag.
Neither does traveling with them. Here's how to
make sure they end up at the same place you do.

Packing your bags

➤ Never pack these items in any bag you plan to check: money, passport, keys, camera, jewelry, medicine, glass, perishables or irreplaceables.

➤ Always pack those items — plus any personal things you'll need for 48 hours — in a carry-on bag that will fit under your airline seat or in the overhead bin. Call the airline and ask what that means in inches.

➤ Hazardous items are prohibited, and airlines define these broadly: aerosols (like hairsprays), flammables, cigarette lighters, filled divers' tanks and many solvents. Even loose matches are allowed only in your pockets. Call beforehand about transporting anything questionable.

➤ Ask about the limits on the number of bags, total weight of your bags and odd-sized containers.

➤ Attach sturdy luggage tags to your bags. Mark them with the address and phone number of your *business* or *destination* — never your home — which billboards its vacancy for burglars.

➤ Shield rolls of film from airport X-rays by packing them in lead-lined bags, available at your camera store.

➤ Diskettes and other magnetic media do not

need to be protected from the X-ray machine, but can be ruined by the metal detector. Send them through the conveyor.

➤ Put your business cards inside your luggage. Tear off all tags from previous trips.

➤ Always lock your bags securely — use padlocks. Don't rely on flimsy built-in locks. Use straps if the clasps or hinges are weak.

➤ Put brightly colored tape on the outside so you can spot your bags easily as they zoom by on the carousel.

➤ At check-in, be certain they put a tag on each of your bags showing the correct three-letter code to your destination airport — plus any connecting airports. If you don't know the codes, ask.

➤ Make sure they hand you one claim check for each bag. Hold onto all claim checks until you've retrieved your bags and verified that everything's still in them and undamaged.

Shipping oddities

Sensitive Equipment. To bring stereos, computers, appliances or large musical instruments with you, protect them in padded hard-shell cases or in original factory cartons. Cover any markings of their contents so you don't tempt thieves, and label them "fragile." Always ask about the airline's liability policy.

Animals. Policies and fees differ, but all airlines need advance notice. Go to your veterinarian for the required health certificate and recommendations to ensure your pet's well-being. Guide dogs are exempt from most animal restrictions — see page 82.

Bikes, Skis, Etc. Call the airline in advance.

Shipping tricks

The BackSaver. A week or two before your domestic flight, insure and ship your items by mail or UPS to your destination. Always tell the recipient to expect your package. If it's going to a hotel, write "hold for guest arrival" on the outside. Save the box to ship things back at the end of your trip.

The BikeSaver. Pay a neighborhood bike shop to pack up your two-wheeler and ship it, insured, to a bike shop near your destination. Have it reassembled when you arrive.

Reuniting with your luggage

- ➤ Be careful not to walk off with bags that look like yours. Check the luggage tags to be sure.
- ➤ If you're the last one left when the carousel stops, check with the baggage claim office.
- ➤ If your bags aren't there, fill out the missing luggage form, *even if they say your luggage should arrive on the next flight.* Keep a copy of the form, and write down your claim check numbers, the agent's name and a *direct* phone number.
- ➤ Until your bags are found, some airlines provide you with a cash advance — the amount is nego-

tiable. Others will reimburse you for reasonable expenses. Hold onto your receipts.

➤ If your checked luggage or its contents are lost, damaged or stolen, you are entitled to compensation. The small print on your ticket spells out money limits, and items not covered.

➤ If your bag is damaged, torn or open, check immediately to see if any items are missing. Fill out the paperwork *before* you leave the airport, get a copy of the form, the agent's name and a *direct* phone number.

➤ If you discover later that items are missing, call the airline immediately. Take notes on the who/what/when/where of your call. Follow up with a certified letter.

➤ If your bag is lost, you'll have to negotiate with the airline for the amount of compensation. For more information, or if you are dissatisfied with their offer, see page 152.

➤ Don't panic. Most bags are found within 2 to 48 hours, and the airline will usually deliver them to wherever you're staying.

Top Things That Make Flight Attendants Crabby

Or what not to do to get good service.

Your flight attendant is a professional trained to handle many emergencies, most of which you'll never see. Here are the things that inconsiderate people do to drive them batty during average flights.

- ✈ Send food "back to the chef."
- ✈ Shove aside the aisle cart to get to the lavatory.
- ✈ Ring the call button for magazines during meal service.
- ✈ Ask if a lavatory is vacant when the OCCUPIED sign is on.
- ✈ Enter the service galley thinking it's a lavatory.
- ✈ Hand them a freshly used diaper.
- ✈ Ask them to repeat the whole list of drinks — then order a Coke.
- ✈ Yank off the wall ashtray to open the lavatory door.
- ✈ Make them guess, when they ask what you'd like to drink.
- ✈ Make passes at them. From the window seat.
- ✈ Blame them for flight delays.
- ✈ Don't return a smile.
- ✈ Don't say thank you.

Heard any good ones lately? Jot 'em down and send 'em in. See page 156 for the address.

Tickets Please

Airline tickets can read like alphabet soup to the average traveler. Of those entries you *can* read, make sure the following are correct: your name, airline, flight numbers, dates and all connecting flights. It must say "OK" in the status box on each page, or your reservation is *not* confirmed. Call the airline's toll-free number if you have any questions.

They'll detach one page for each leg of your journey — make sure they don't remove two sheets by mistake. The last page is your passenger coupon and receipt. Keep all pages together safely in the ticket folder, along with baggage claim checks and boarding passes. *Always protect your tickets like cash.*

If you lose your ticket

Call the airline immediately — and hope no one else has used it. You may have to pay a lost ticket fee, wait forever for a refund, and pay the current going rate for a replacement ticket. You'll be better off if you can give them the ticket's serial number, or show them a photocopy of your ticket.

Connecting Flights

As the plane descends into your connecting city, here's how to minimize the mad-dash hassle through the airport:

➤ Listen for the crew's announcement of your arrival and connecting gates — or ask. Write them on your ticket envelope.

➤ Check the airport diagram in the back of your in-flight magazine to locate these gates. It's okay to take the magazine with you.

➤ The airline will automatically transfer your luggage to your connecting flight.

➤ Check in at the connecting gate as soon as possible — *never assume you have plenty of time.*

➤ If there is extra time after you check in, call an old friend in that city. It's a local call!

➤ Ask the ticket agent if you get a meal on your next flight — and don't spoil your appetite.

➤ Enjoy the people parade. Read the hometown paper. Put your luggage in a security locker and take a walk.

Stranded!

Being stranded after missing a connection doesn't mean a lavish hotel room or sumptuous dinner — unless you're buying. The facts are, nothing is required by law, and each airline has its own policies. Here's the scoop:

➤If your initial flight is delayed — and you're certain to miss your connection — immediately ask the airline to change your connection to a later flight.

➤If your flight is cancelled at the last minute, go right to a pay phone and call the airline's toll-free reservation number. It's quicker than standing in line at the ticket counter.

➤If you miss a connection, or a flight is cancelled, the airline should try to seat you on its next available flight. If that's not possible, some will try to seat you on another airline. Or you may be entitled to a refund if you choose not to go.

➤If the delay or cancellation is caused by the airline — such as mechanical problems — you may be entitled to amenities such as free meals, lodging and long-distance calls.

➤ If the delay or cancellation is caused by something beyond the airline's control — like weather — you may be on your own, stuck in the airport with everyone else.

➤ If you miss the flight — and it's your fault — many airlines will try to seat you on their next flight to your destination. But there's no rules, guarantees or compensation. So be nice.

➤ If your flight is diverted to another city, ask for basic amenities if they're not offered.

Be sure to speak up — pleasantly but firmly — for services you believe you're entitled to. Airline agents are often given leeway to offer compensation if you make a good case. Not satisfied? Have them get out their *"Conditions of Carriage"* and show you where it says they can't do it. Still not satisfied? Save all out-of-pocket expense receipts. Turn to page 152.

The Joys Of Being Bumped

Imagine arriving in time for check-in only to discover your confirmed seat has just been given to someone else. The airline overbooked your flight. Legally!

Would a juicy reward for getting "bumped" to a later flight calm you down? Although the fine print on overbooking and compensation varies among airlines, they're all required to ask for volunteers first.

If you're a bumpee wannabe

Time on your hands? Looking for freebies? Listen for the call for volunteers to give up their seats, and find out what's offered in return. Although they're not required by law to give you anything, virtually all airlines will.

Remember, compensation is *negotiable* and can depend on how many seats they need to free up, and how many volunteers are competing. Compensation usually means cash or free tickets. Just make sure you get a *confirmed* seat on the next flight to your destination.

If you're an involuntary bumpee

As long as the airline can fly you to your destination within one hour of your originally scheduled arrival time, they'll call it even.

Beyond that, you're immediately entitled to the value of a one-way ticket for delays up to two hours, or twice that amount for longer delays in addition to keeping your original ticket. But there's lots of fine print: these amounts have maximum limits, you must have had a confirmed seat, have met their check-in deadline, and much more. Further, there's no compensation if weather or a safety condition forced them to change planes or cancel the flight. Ask to see the written statement of your rights. Know there's always room for negotiation. And if you're still dissatisfied, go to page 152.

International Travel Tips

From the moment you step on foreign soil, you become an alien. No, you won't suddenly sprout Spock ears or want to phone home. But you will be subject to very different laws. In advance of your trip, learn as much as possible about the foreign country's entry and exit requirements. Get answers by calling its embassy or consulate in your own country before leaving. Here are a few more suggestions:

➤ Call the U.S. State Department for up-to-date recorded travel information on every country in the world, including health requirements, currency changes, civil unrest warnings and other important facts. Call 24-hours a day: (202) 647-5225 or modem up the computer bulletin board: (202) 647-9225.

➤ Make sure your passport is up to date, and will not expire while you're traveling.

➤ Ask your travel agent if you'll need a visa — a country's authorization to enter. Some countries require visas for short visits; most require them for stays over three months. Don't wait until the last minute. It can take several weeks to obtain one, and there may be a fee.

➤ If a landing card is required, most airlines will give you one before arrival. Fill it out on the plane and save time on the ground. Hold on to any receipt they hand you — you may need it when you leave the country.

➤ Preserve your passport in a clear plastic protector. This also provides a built-in pocket for important travel papers and landing-card receipts. If you lose your passport, call your embassy or consulate immediately. They can also help you in case of illness or injury.

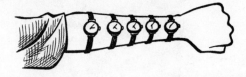

➤ Always bring small bills in local currency to use for tips and taxi fare on arrival. Just try to get change from your fifty from a bellhop in Bologna.

➤ Most airports around the world now use international graphic symbols on their signs, so you don't have to worry about getting around till you're out of the airport.

Flights of Fantasy

With all those years of passenger service, the airlines still haven't come up with some of the extras that can *really* make flying a pleasure. Here are our suggestions — if you can top 'em, see page 156.

- ✈ Intercom Karaoke.
- ✈ **Walk-in luggage closets.**
- ✈ Picture windows.
- ✈ **A mute button for pilot prattle.**
- ✈ Coffee, tea, margaritas.
- ✈ **More than 5 peanuts per bag.**
- ✈ All-U-can-eat salad bars.
- ✈ **Movies you haven't seen yet.**
- ✈ Domino's deliveries.
- ✈ **Refunds for turbulence.**
- ✈ Fines for snorers.
- ✈ **Hot showers. Hot tubs. Hot pastrami.**
- ✈ Broadway musicals in the aisles.
- ✈ **Laz-E-Boy seats in coach.**
- ✈ Goose-down pillows.
- ✈ **Electric blankets.**
- ✈ A REAL chef.
- ✈ **A REAL omelet.**
- ✈ A REAL steak.
- ✈ **In-flight laundry service.**
- ✈ Ejection seats for obnoxious passengers.
- ✈ **Your very own arm rests.**

Someone Special In The Air.

Smart flying ideas for:

Flying Youngsters

Kids on planes cry, run, holler, fight and spill. Weary flight attendants mutter that some kids do everything but sleep. Here are some secrets for happy flights with kids.

In advance

➤ Build enthusiasm for the trip: take a pre-flight tour of the airport. Emphasize the fun parts of the trip.

➤ Request to sit in the bulkhead — the first seats in any section of the plane — where there's more

floor space, and you may be closer to the restrooms.

➤ Babies under two usually fly free if they sit on your lap. If you choose to secure them in a safety seat, you'll have to pay the fare. For information on child seating, write to the FAA. See page 154.

➤ Book your return for at least a day before school begins, to give them time to readjust.

➤ Ask about special kids' meals, airport activity rooms and on-board entertainment kits.

➤ If you're bringing a stroller, call the airline to be sure it can be brought on board.

Day of the flight

➤ Dress for comfort. Carry extra diapers and a change of clothes for baby and you, in case unexpected things come up.

➤ Create a light-weight fun bag with favorite snacks, simple toys and a few surprises. Include a bottle of water, a sweater and important medication — enough to sustain them if you had a 24-hour luggage delay. Pack a favorite toy, unless it's a toy gun.

➤ Be sure to put a luggage tag on the busy-bag.

On the plane

➤ Take advantage of pre-boarding privileges. Use the quiet time to get settled.

➤ Babies and small children cry on take-off and landing because of air pressure changes that hurt their ears. This is the time to start a bottle, get out the pacifier, or hand out chewing gum.

➤ Never hand a dirty diaper to the flight attendant. Seal it in an airsickness bag and dispose of it in the proper lavatory trash bin.

➤ Play it safe — control your kid. The aisle is not a playground, and your child could get hurt.

Upon arrival

➤ The baggage carousel looks like a fun carnival ride, but it's dangerous. Keep kids away!

➤ If you're traveling alone with an active toddler, consider a waist-to-waist tether. A few glances from nosy passers-by are worth ensuring your child's safety in a busy airport.

➤ Spring for the extra buck — rent a luggage cart. Make your life easier. A backpack toddler tote will free your hands.

O.P.A.K. (Other People's Annoying Kids)

➤ You can't shut 'em up or hypnotize 'em, but you can divert 'em.

➤ Carry a few inexpensive child-safe plastic toys to give to aggravating kids. Or give 'em the comics from your paper. It's cheap self-defense.

➤ Be sure to ask the parent first — most kids are properly taught not to accept goodies from strangers.

Kids: Not-Home Alone

Airlines transport thousands of children traveling by themselves every year. It can be scarier for parents than for kids; but if it's necessary for your child to fly alone, do it right:

In advance

➤ Tell the airline your child will be traveling alone and request a nonstop or direct flight. Ask about age requirements, assistance and special forms you'll need to fill out. Be sure to check the policies of any connecting airlines.

Day of the flight

➤ Make three copies of your child's identification and flight plans, plus the name, address and phone number of the person meeting her. Place a copy in her carry-on bag, in her luggage and on her, along with some cash and coins for the phone.

➤ Arrive early to fill out forms. Introduce your child to the flight crew. Stay at the gate till the plane takes off. Tell the person meeting your child to arrive at the airport early, and to bring identification.

Savings For Seniors

Seniors today have more time and money to travel than ever before, and they represent one of the fastest-growing segments in the travel business. For getting great deals, people 62 or over win hands-down. Each major U.S. airline offers deep-discount fares for seniors, usually in the form of coupon books. You purchase these coupons at a discount, and later redeem them for flights, which come with fewer restrictions and a year-long price freeze. The savings are amazing, but ask around: deals vary depending on the airline. Coupon books are cost-effective only if you plan on taking two or more domestic trips a year, and the airline serves the cities you wish to visit. Keep in mind that special deals can change overnight. For more information, contact your travel agent or the individual airline.

Grown-ups Going It Alone

Even if you've logged more miles than Sally Ride, don't assume you're above it all. Flying alone means you have to think on your feet. Review these important pre-flight safety checks and keep flying with confidence.

➤ Register with a friend: give someone your itinerary, phone numbers where you can be reached and when you're due back.

➤ Lighten your wallet or purse before you go. Take out unnecessary membership and department store credit cards, office pass-keys, etc. But be sure to leave in your driver's license and auto club card — even if you don't plan to drive.

➤ Be aware of your surroundings. Follow your instincts. Never ask strangers to watch your things.

➤ If you don't wish to speak to your seatmate, wear headphones. You don't even need a tape player — just tuck the wire into your pocket.

Extra tips for savvy women . . .

- ➤ Don't display your good jewelry, or you'll be a target for thieves. Leave the good stuff at home.

- ➤ Walk with a sense of purpose — like you have no time to be bothered.

- ➤ Bring only as much as you can carry comfortably — luggage on wheels helps. Being overladen makes you vulnerable.

- ➤ Married or not, consider wearing a wedding ring. It may not repel hardcore wolves, but it sends a message that you don't want to be bothered.

- ➤ Memorize a few phrases in some obscure language. Unwelcome strangers can be told, "Garbage in season is riper at home" in Phoenician. Stops 'em cold.

- ➤ At check-in, you can ask to be seated next to another female passenger.

- ➤ In public restrooms, don't hang your purse on the hooks inside the door. A thief can lift it from the other side, and you're in no position to give chase.

- ➤ Pregnant women should check with their doctor and the airline about potential restrictions. Pack healthy snacks, and book an aisle seat for easy lavatory access.

Business Productivity Guide

Turn flying time into billable time. Here are a few tips to help you bring your satellite office up to speed:

➤ Have your priority items packed near the top of your briefcase or carry-on, for easier access at your seat.

➤ Instead of writing long memos, speak softly into a micro-cassette recorder.

➤ Take advantage of the latest generation of air phones, modems and fax hook-ups, now available on many commercial planes. Bill 'em to the client.

➤ If there are individual touch-sensitive video screens on board, you'll be able to check stock quotes, get sports scores, obtain connecting gate information — even play video games.

➤ If your brain power is low, you can still put the time to good use: fill out expense reports, write postcards, make lists of things to do, gifts to buy, etc.

➤ Don't start a game or a conversation with an unescorted child, unless you want to play surrogate parent for the rest of the flight.

➤ For fewer distractions, avoid sitting in the bulkhead — especially from May to September, where unescorted children usually sit.

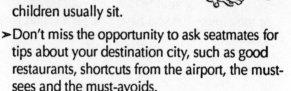

➤ Don't miss the opportunity to ask seatmates for tips about your destination city, such as good restaurants, shortcuts from the airport, the must-sees and the must-avoids.

➤ Even if you can't get any solid work done, use the time for rethinking problems, setting goals, developing creative strategies and brainstorming.

➤ Consider joining your airline's airport club or visiting an on-site business service center, for more comfort and business amenities while you're waiting in airports.

Travelers With Disabilities

When a person with a disability needs to fly, U.S. airlines are required to accommodate most everyone. The rules are too numerous to cover here — just be aware that a lot depends on specific circumstances. To help ensure a smooth flight:

➤When booking your tickets, tell your travel agent or the airline that you have a disability, and what it is.

> Contact the airports where you will travel —
> including any connecting airports — and make
> special arrangements, such as for a wheelchair.

> If you are not accommodated like any other
> passenger, ask to speak to the Complaint
> Resolution Officer immediately to help resolve
> your problem.

Free information

To get the facts on specific laws, accessibility
features and complaint procedures, send for:

> *New Horizons for the Air Traveler with a Disability.*
> U.S. Department of Transportation, I-25,
> 400 7th St., SW, Washington, DC 20590, or call
> (202) 366-2220, or TT (202) 755-7687.

> *Access Travel: Airports,* featuring a list of the
> services and accessible design features of more
> than 500 airports worldwide. Consumer Informa-
> tion Center, P.O. Box 100, Pueblo, CO 81002.

> *Resource information sheets,* or for general
> questions, write to the Society for the
> Advancement of Travel for the Handicapped,
> 347 Fifth Ave., Suite 610, New York, NY 10016,
> or call (212) 447-7284.

For Your Safety & Comfort.

If you think the crew's pre-flight announcement is a good time to start the crossword, then you should have no trouble coming up with a seven-letter word for someone who doesn't show good sense.

Sure, you may have heard the safety briefing dozens of times over the years. So let's see you ace the pop quiz on page 87.

Even though you're about 19 times safer on a scheduled airliner than you are on an interstate highway, you have to know the rules of safe air travel. They can save your life:

➤ Follow — don't question — all instructions given to you by the flight crew. They're for your own safety.

➤ Ask yourself: exactly how many rows am I from each emergency exit. If I were to wear a blindfold, could I find my way directly to all of them?

➤ Fasten your safety belt snugly around your hips — not your stomach. Keep it fastened even if the captain turns off the seatbelt sign.

➤Have you pushed your carry-on bags completely
  under the seat in front of you?

➤Take a moment now to familiarize yourself with
  the operation of your safety belt, life vest and
  oxygen mask. Know where to find the flotation
  equipment. Read the safety card in the seat pocket
  in front of you. If you have any questions, ask.

In case of emergency

➤Keep your wits about you. Do exactly what the
  trained flight crew tells you to do.

Answers to Safety Quiz

1, 2, 3, 5 = True

4 = False

Safety Quiz

Just when you think it's safe to snooze, here comes that pesky pre-flight safety demo. You've heard it so often, you can probably recite it in your sleep. Well let's just see, shall we?

Circle True or False:

1. **T or F** Not all planes have the oxygen mask located in the overhead compartment.

2. **T or F** If you're traveling with a child, place the oxygen mask over your own mouth first, and *then* attend to the child's mask.

3. **T or F** Emergency exit doors may operate differently, depending on the aircraft.

4. **T or F** Flotation devices are inflated by using the bicycle pump located under the armrest.

5. **T or F** Floor lights along the aisles will guide you to all emergency exits.

Scoring: 100% correct: **A+**   0–99% correct: **F**

see me after the flight.

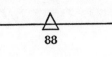
If You Feel Panicky Right Now

Breathe In.

Count to three.

Breathe Out.

Count to three.

Breathe and Count.

Breathe and Count.

Do this over and over until it makes a
rhythm and your heartbeat is more normal.

If you can, read on. If not, just keep
breathing and counting — that's just fine.

If you like, someone can read this to
you, slowly, as you are ready for
each section.

You Are In Control

Panic attacks are really about feeling in control.

YOU ARE IN CONTROL.

More than it feels like, you are.

Feel your back against the seat.

Feel your feet on the floor, and your arms on the armrests.

You are on a journey you planned, to a destination YOU chose. This is very good.

You are close to trained people who will help you if you need it.

BREATHE IN. Count to three.

BREATHE OUT.

THIS MOMENT WILL PASS.

Put your hands on the edges of the arm-rests, and squeeze as tight as you like; then deliberately release and rest. No one will notice. You can send your feelings into the seat arms: press, count to three and release, press, count to three and release. Make the rhythm the same as your breathing.

You Are Safe, And Doing Better

Every time you breathe out, send a bit of tension out with the tide of your breath.

Every time you count to three, use that count to send the tension into the outgoing breath. Layer it on the stream of air, just like buttering a piece of bread, and send it out of you.

As long as you sit still and quiet in your seat, no one will notice.

Breathe in, count to three, breathe a little tension out.

If you want to, call the attendant.
They are trained to assist you, and they
will be there for you if you need them.

THIS MOMENT WILL PASS.

BREATHE IN, COUNT TO THREE.

BREATHE THE FEELINGS OUT.

Mental Field Trips.

Take a breather with this

guided tour of your

mental landscape.

Mental field trip guidelines

Hypnotherapists use guided visualizations for everything from improving golf games to calming fears. The mind doesn't distinguish between reality and imagination when it comes to physical reaction. That's why visualizing a juicy sour bright yellow lemon touching your tongue can make you salivate — vivid thoughts FEEL real to your mind. See?

These visualizations can assist your flexibility on a long flight, and even keep your feet from swelling. Read through one mental field trip until you have the gist of it, then put down the book and take your tour.

Mental Field Trip #1

Sit up straight, legs uncrossed, feet flat on the floor, and close your eyes. In your mind, see a place where you walk — your favorite park, the smooth marble floors of a well-lit shopping mall, the long halls at work . . . any place.

Put yourself in that setting, ready to walk, and begin.

Follow a path that pleases you: look at the flowers, watch the dogs playing, scope out the shops with the best bargains, see which co-workers' doors are open, and what each is doing in the offices. Internally narrate the tour to yourself or to a walking buddy (wanna stroll with Einstein or Madonna? It's your visualization, have it any way you want it!). Feel your tendons stretching and your ankles working. Feel your calf muscles elongating to accommodate slight slopes, and see yourself adjusting your speed and stride as you walk.

Rehearsing in your mind has total psychological validity, and can keep you from stiffening up in your seat. Side effects from a "walk" like this can include a clearer head and a better frame of mind.

Mental Field Trip #2

Close your eyes and visualize your feet and legs in your mind's eye. See the skin, the scars, the beauty marks — make sure these are YOUR legs.

Now, in your mind, give yourself a foot massage. Start with your toes on one foot. Rub the ball of your foot, the instep, the heel, the inside and outside of your ankle. Imagine your hands applying gentle pressure to the top and bottom of your foot, then up the calf. Feel the sensations of what you "see" your hands doing. Now, do the other foot.

Make sure your massage begins at the toes and works up your leg. Take three minutes to imagine this each hour, or as often as you like. This mental foot massage can keep your feet from swelling during the flight.

Carry-On Mood-Boosters

Assume the best, but pack for the worst. Your carry-on can provide a smorgasbord of satisfying in-flight solutions.

➤**Snacks.** Don't assume airlines always feed you. Bring your own favorite foods, and avoid the temptation to bring fatty and salty treats. Good snacks to pack: unsalted nuts, dried or fresh fruits, veggies, and low-fat mini-cheeses sealed in wax.

➤**Après Snacks.** A toothbrush and minty toothpaste are a cheap, easy way to reassert your sense of well-being, as well as de-furring your mouth.

➤**Overcome Dry Airplane Air.** Sample-sized bottles of unscented hand lotion and saline nasal spray will keep you comfortable. Drinking lots of water will keep you rehydrated.

➤**Stronger Than Hurt.** Don't be held up by a midair toothache or airport-store prices. Ibuprofen is an exceptional painkiller. Bring your own. Or ask the flight attendant.

- ➤ **I Vant To Be Alone.** Very dark sunglasses are great for snoozing. People may think you're a film star.

- ➤ **Bedroom Slippers.** Unless you're being followed by paparazzi, wear them on the plane. Changing your heel height can give you a new attitude.

On-The-Spot Remedies

Away from your medicine cabinet, any ache can be agony. A couple of trade secrets can go a long way towards easing discomforts in the privacy of your seat.

Acupressure — Full-Court Press Against Pain

Acupressure is the stimulation of specific points along your body's energy channels, and it works whether you believe in it or not. Ask the billions of Chinese who have used it for thousands of years.

Simply trying it uses your time constructively — it costs nothing, requires no equipment and creates no side effects. You have nothing to lose but your pain.

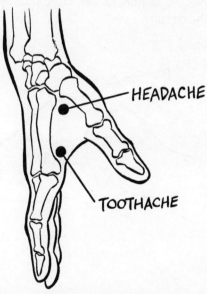

HEADACHE

TOOTHACHE

Cure Your Headache

There's an acupressure point named Hegu (the
Yuan-Source point, if you're into Oriental medicine
trivia) on the fleshy part of your hand, between your
thumb and forefinger. To find it, move your left
thumb up into the 'V' between the bones of your
right thumb and right forefinger, as far up as it will
go without hitting the bone (see illustration). Press
on that spot — not hard enough to hurt — just
medium pressure until the headache goes away.
To assist the healing further, close your eyes and
breathe deeply.

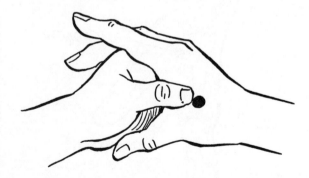

Relieve Your Toothache

Serious dental problems will feel worse on a plane. You may be surprised by a cavity you didn't know you had, or a chronic twinge that turns out to be an excruciating abscess after takeoff. It's a good idea not to fly within 12 hours of dental work.

Find Sanjian, the Shu-Stream point, by first finding the headache point with your thumb, and then backing off half-way along the forefinger bone. When you make a loose fist, the toothache point is right next to the end of the bone in your hand that connects with your forefinger (see illustration on page 103). Press forcefully until the pain begins to diminish. Closing your eyes, clearing your mind and breathing deeply will assist this process.

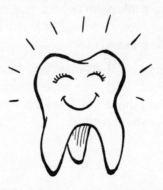

Keeping Lunch

If you're having a little trouble catching a full breath, or your stomach is uneasy, try this.

Feel for the acupressure point above your inner wrist, two fingers' width up your arm above the crease and between the tendons. Press this as though you were taking a pulse. Close your eyes, breathe deeply and focus on the air cleansing your system as it goes in and out of your lungs.

An alternative stomach-settling point can be found on the crease of your inner elbow. Roll up your sleeve and bend your arm slightly to see the crease, and feel the tendon in the middle of the bend. This point is on the inner side of the tendon, just below where your biceps muscle begins (see illustration). Press this point as hard as is comfortable, close your eyes, breathe deeply and focus on your breath going in and out.

These two points will regulate your heartbeat, calm your stomach and release the tension in your elbows, arms and shoulders. The elbow-point can also help relieve dry-mouth.

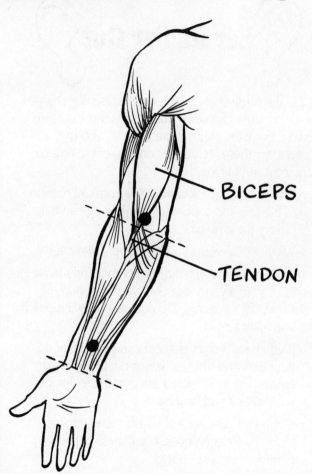

BICEPS

TENDON

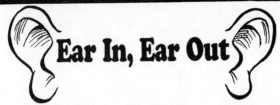

Ear In, Ear Out

As the plane changes altitude, the resulting changes in air pressure can wreak havoc on your eardrums. Even though the cabin is pressurized, you may still need to try these techniques on descent to reduce stuffiness in your ears:

➤ Chew gum or suck candy. The constant motion of the jaw and continued swallowing can help relieve the pressure.

➤ Yawn. Force yourself. Then keep yawning.

➤ Pinch your nostrils shut, then very gently blow out through your nose until your ears pop. Repeat as necessary. Do not use this technique if you have a cold.

➤ If you have a cold, descent can be tougher on your ears and sinuses. Take a decongestant or nasal spray so its effects are timed to coincide with takeoff and landing.

➤ If you ears still aren't clear after landing, keep trying these techniques. If stuffiness or pain continue, see your doctor.

Fearless Flying

Experts say more than one-out-of-six adult Americans has some fear of flying. This can keep people from attending far-away weddings of loved ones, or accepting higher-paying jobs where air travel is required.

If you have fears, they can be overcome in most cases. When you learn more about the safety of air travel, how an aircraft lifts off the ground, and what an airplane's noises mean, you can relax — which automatically eases anxiety (pages 24-31).

Redirecting your thoughts to comforting personal images can help you relax, too (pages 94-99). And learning a few simple breathing techniques can help you stay calm and composed (pages 88-93).

Several airlines and private clinics offer afford-able weekend or evening programs to help you fly without fear, and they claim a very high success rate. Ask your travel agent to recommend one of these worthwhile programs, and call for free information. You really *can* learn to fly fearlessly.

Kicking Jet Lag

How to beat the body-clock blues.

Fatigue. Insomnia. Disorientation. Loss of appetite. No, it's not love, it's jet lag. You can get it when you fly across several time zones, and your body rhythms need a few days — or weeks — to catch up. Jet lag is normal, but it's distressing when you're at an 8 a.m. breakfast meeting and your brain insists you should still be in bed.

The good news is that you won't be jet lagged when you fly north or south — just tired. But jet lag will compound your flying fatigue on any east-west flight that crosses time zones — even one.

Doctors and sleep specialists are still learning better ways to beat jet lag so you can arrive feeling

refreshed. There are a number of remedies available now, from diet adjustment to sunlight therapy, and they may or may not work for you. Your travel agent or librarian can point you in the right direction, but the best advice will come from your physician. The idea is to trick your body into resetting its internal clock. Here are a few tips to get you started:

- ➤ Skip caffeine the day of your flight, and eat lightly if at all while you're in the air. Don't gorge yourself on all those free meals and desserts.

- ➤ Avoid all alcohol. Drink lots of water and juice.

- ➤ Book your flight later in the day so you can sleep on the plane and arrive after dark.

- ➤ To stay alert when your body wants to sleep, go out into the sunlight. Don't nap.

- ➤ Set your watch for your destination, and do what the locals do. If it's suppertime, eat a light supper, even if your body says it's bedtime.

- ➤ If you require medicine for chronic conditions, consult your doctor about adjustments to medication and eating schedules.

- ➤ Try not to make any major decisions for at least 24 hours after landing — you won't be at your best.

Quick Pick-Me-Ups

Try these in-flight feel-good ideas from frequent
flyers — and the people who serve them.

➤ Wear your most comfortable shoes. If you must
  wear dress shoes, remove them — feet and
  ankles swell from long periods of inactivity.
  Carry a shoe horn to get them back on.

➤ Loosen ties, belts and other restrictive clothing.
  Ask your flight attendant for pillows — place one
  behind your head and one supporting your
  lower back.

➤ In-flight temperatures can vary considerably.
  Dress lightly — it's easier to ask for a blanket
  than to remove excess clothing.

➤ Drink lots of water or juice to counteract dehy-
  dration. Avoid carbonated drinks...you can't
  blame it on the dog. Go easy on coffee and
  alcohol — they only dehydrate you more.

➤ Eat lightly. Just say no to that second free meal
  on a connecting flight.

➤ Since the air in the plane is dry, you'll feel better wearing glasses instead of contact lenses.

➤ Relieve the strain on your back. Keep your knees higher than your hips by putting a briefcase or small carry-on under your feet.

➤ Get some shut-eye. Use an eye shade if necessary. Bring an inflatable U-shaped travel pillow for your neck. For sleeping upright, it works like a dream!

➤ Give yourself lots of room to stretch your legs. Put your carry-on in the overhead bin if you won't need it during the flight. You can also get more legroom by reserving a seat in the emergency exit rows — but you must be willing to accept the added responsibilities. Ask the ticket agent or flight attendant. If you've got the extra bucks, go first class.

➤ Get up and walk around once in a while. Try the stretching exercises on the following pages.

Seat S·t·r·e·t·c·h·i·n·g

Even seasoned couch potatoes have trouble sitting for long flights. There's no TV to stare at, no refrigerator to go to, and not even a couch to lie down on.

But there is one way to limber up while you relieve the boredom and stiffness of a long transcontinental or overseas flight: *stretch*. It gets your blood circulating, and helps you feel invigorated, especially after napping.

You can do some great stretching and flexing exercises right in your seat — without getting looks from other passengers. Remember to go slow and easy — small movements work just fine. Your goal is gentle stretching, not grunts, flailing or breaking a sweat. And be sure to take a short walk through the plane every couple of hours.

You can try the following five exercises right in your seat. If your seatmates look puzzled, do them a favor: show them this book so they can flex out, too!

The Yabba Dabba II

Pretend you're driving the Flintstones' car and 'jog' the plane across Bedrock.

Then rotate your feet at the ankles, first clockwise, then counterclockwise. Do the same with your wrists.

Let's Neck

Keeping your shoulders down, turn your head to the right, and stretch ear-to-shoulder. Repeat on the left side.

Then, with the same motion, stretch your *chin* over your right shoulder. Repeat on left side.

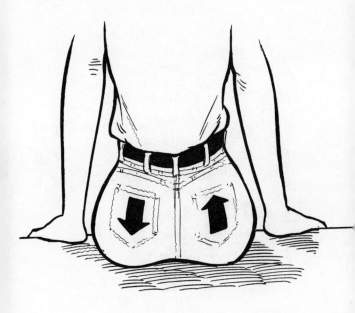

The Bun Warmer

Keep the beat with your cheeks. Alternately tense and relax your right and left gluteus maximus muscles, in time with the music on the headset.

The "I Dunno"

Shrug, as if someone just asked if you know the square root of 873. Bring your shoulders up to your ears, and then lower them as far as they'll go. Feels good, huh? So do it again.

The Annoyer

Clasp your hands behind your head, and pull your elbows back toward the seat, squeezing your shoulder blades closer together. Relax and repeat.

Smoking Section

If you're a smoker, your life changed dramatically on February 25, 1990, when smoking was banned from virtually all commercial scheduled flights over the continental United States.

If it burns you up that the NO-SMOKING sign can light up — but you can't — these suggestions might help:

➤ Program yourself in advance to use the time constructively and focus on things you enjoy. Read a positive-message book, write letters, listen to music, do the crossword, watch the movie. Book the red-eye next time and sleep.

➤ Stay away from things that are linked to smoking in your mind: sipping coffee, lingering over dessert, drinking alcohol, talking on the airphone, etc.

➤ For mouth attention, chew gum or suck candy. This will help clear your ears on descent, too.

➤ No matter how tempting, remember there's a smoke detector in the lavatory — and a stiff penalty for disabling it.

Your Last-Minute Flight Check.

You won't need *everything* from home to feel at home — just the good stuff. Pick 'n' choose from these lists. And if you travel frequently, keep a bag ready to go, with everything in sample sizes.

Essentials Checklist

- ☐ Passport/citizenship proof
- ☐ Airline tickets
- ☐ Airline VIP card
- ☐ Vaccination certificates
- ☐ Map of where you're going
- ☐ Foreign language phrase book
- ☐ Security wallet or moneybelt
- ☐ Pocket compass
- ☐ Comfortable old walking shoes
- ☐ Extra eyeglasses/reading glasses/contacts
- ☐ Sunglasses
- ☐ Wouldn't-hurt-to-lose-it watch
- ☐ Empty tote bag to bring back souvenirs
- ☐ Folding umbrella
- ☐ Conversion tables: metric, money, etc.
- ☐ Notebook and dependable pen
- ☐ Adapters for foreign currents/outlets
- ☐ Camera, film and lead-lined bag
- ☐ Personal stereo and music
- ☐ Small flashlight
- ☐ Batteries: camera, flashlight, calculator, hearing aid

Packing Personal Stuff

You know what you need — slip this stuff in with it. Tighten screw-tops, so nothing oozes. Zipper-lock bags are a blessing. Carry on what you can't live without.

- ☐ Travel alarm clock
- ☐ Nail clipper/file
- ☐ Cotton swabs
- ☐ Styptic pencil
- ☐ Skin moisturizer
- ☐ Lip balm
- ☐ Sunscreen
- ☐ Toothpaste, brush, floss
- ☐ Comb, hairbrush
- ☐ Shampoo, conditioner
- ☐ Deodorant
- ☐ Perfume/cologne/aftershave
- ☐ Disposable toilet seat covers
- ☐ Tampons/sanitary protection
- ☐ Cold-water fabric wash
- ☐ Individual moist towelettes
- ☐ Tissue pack
- ☐ Clean underwear
- ☐ Condoms, because these are the '90's

Will You Be Sorry If You Don't Have . . .

- ☐ Chewing gum for ear-pressure relief
- ☐ Sleeping pills
- ☐ Motion-sickness remedy
- ☐ Neck pillow
- ☐ Spare contact lenses
- ☐ Foam shoe insoles
- ☐ Bathroom tissue
- ☐ Travel hair drier
- ☐ Travel iron
- ☐ Travel shoeshine kit
- ☐ Shoehorn
- ☐ Sleep shades
- ☐ Book to read
- ☐ Swimsuit

Most Emergencies Can Be Fixed With . . .

- ☐ Aspirin/ibuprofen/Tylenol
- ☐ Clear nail polish
- ☐ Duct tape
- ☐ Tweezers
- ☐ Safety pins, needle & thread
- ☐ Extension cord
- ☐ Swiss Army knife (with scissors)
- ☐ Crazy Glue

Will You Feel More Secure With . . .

- ☐ All personal prescriptions
- ☐ Antacids
- ☐ Vitamins
- ☐ Eye drops
- ☐ Diarrhea remedy
- ☐ Laxative/fiber therapy
- ☐ Cold/flu remedy
- ☐ Small lint brush
- ☐ Adhesive tape & bandages
- ☐ Antiseptic ointment
- ☐ Dandruff remedy
- ☐ Bug repellent
- ☐ Bug-bite ointment
- ☐ Nasal spray/antihistamines
- ☐ Water purification tablets

Did You Write Down?

- ☐ Confirmation numbers for all reservations: plane, car, hotel, etc.
- ☐ Personal medical summary: allergies, blood type, etc.
- ☐ Travelers check numbers

Taking Care Of Business

- ☐ Business cards
- ☐ Personal calendar
- ☐ Mini-recorder
- ☐ Laptop or notebook computer
- ☐ Phone/fax/extension numbers
- ☐ Long distance calling card
- ☐ Small stapler with extra staples
- ☐ Pocket-sized calculator
- ☐ A pad of stick-on notes
- ☐ Extra letterhead and envelopes
- ☐ Stamps
- ☐ Dragon-mouth killers
- ☐ Paper clips/rubber bands/pencils/etc.

Did You Make Photocopies?

- ☐ Airline ticket, all pages
- ☐ Passport, visa
- ☐ All credit cards, fronts and backs
- ☐ Personal address book
- ☐ Your eyeglass prescription
- ☐ Medical and auto insurance cards

Flying Freebies

You may think your ticket was expensive, but don't forget all the freebies that may come with it!

In-Flight Magazine — They want you to swipe it.

Paper Luggage Tags — Grab a handful.

Frequent Flyer Miles — Sign up now for future rewards.

Soft Drinks and Coffee — Drink all you can.

Peanut Snacks — Your entire salt requirement for the week.

Delicious Meals — Sorry . . . just one to a customer.

Flight & Luggage Insurance — Just pay for your ticket on the right credit card.

Extra Diapers — Proof of baby required.

Aspirin or Tylenol — Proof of headache not required.

Pillows & Blankets — But you gotta give 'em back.

Letterhead, Envelopes, Postcards! — Impress your friends.

Playing Cards, Kid's Gizmos, Coloring Books — Ask the nice attendant.

And now for some real fun . . .

Meet Chuck

In the seatpocket in front of you dwells an ornery and lonely genie whom people often treat poorly. This is your chance to become his friend.

Just fish him out of the pocket and draw in the face on the next page. Then cut or tear out the holes as shown on this diagram. Now he's ready to meet and entertain everyone around you, and maybe he'll even reward each of them with three wishes. Kids love him!

WARNING: DURING EXTREME TURBULENCE,
DO NOT DISTURB CHUCK.

If YOU Owned The Airline

Imagine for a moment that you've just become President and CEO of the airline. Nine-figure salary. Swarms of yes-people. Hot & cold running perks. Your own parking space.

Now take a look around. You've got some important corporate decisions to make.

1 The flight uniforms don't do it for you anymore. Don't be shy. Sketch out that new look you've always wanted them to have. The fashion designer is waiting.

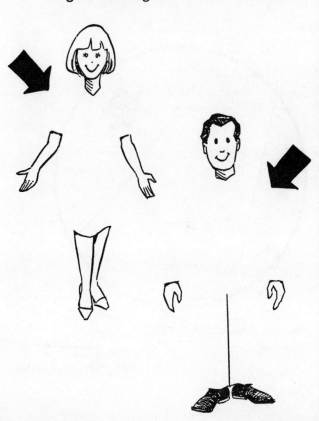

2 You always thought the corporate logo was
   UGLY. Here's your chance to create a bold
   new image — draw it on the side of your planes
   for the world to see. The paint crew is waiting:

3 Passengers keep complaining about the food. You're the boss. Show these whiners how bad it can really get:

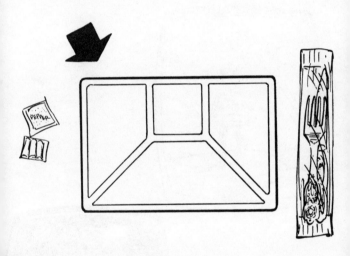

Good work, __ __ (*your initials here*)! You've earned your $1.1 mil for the day. Have your secretary send us your sketches and we'll take care of the rest. Mail them to: CorkScrew Press, 4470-107 Sunset Blvd., Suite 234, Los Angeles, CA 90027.

Scenes You're NOT Likely To See

Jingle Jumble

Many airlines have come and gone, but their slogans, tunes and tag lines live on in our heads forever. Put the trivia section of your brain to work. Give yourself five points for every jingle you can match to its correct airline.

Answer Key

1-G, 2-N, 3-K, 4-E, 5-M, 6-K, 7-I, 8-L, 9-H, 10-J, 11-P, 12-O, 13-B, 14-B, 15-F, 16-M, 17-D, 18-D, 19-G, 20-F, 21-Q, 22-A, 23-C

1. The wings of man.
2. Fly the friendly skies.
3. Makes the going great.
4. We really move our tail for you.
5. Up up and away.
6. World's most experienced airline.
7. Coast to coast to coast.
8. Just plane smart.
9. A passion for perfection.
10. Some people just know how to fly.
11. Take us for all we've got.
12. Begins with you.
13. Something special in the air.
14. Doing what we do best.
15. We love to fly and it shows.
16. Find out how good we really are.
17. We take good care of you.
18. The world's favourite airline.
19. America's favorite way to fly.
20. Ready when you are.
21. The only way to fly.
22. Nobody knows Mexico better.
23. What we serve is you.

A. *Aeroméxico*
B. *American*
C. *America West*
D. *British Airways*
E. *Continental*
F. *Delta*
G. *Eastern*
H. *Lufthansa*
I. *National*
J. *Northwest*
K. *Pan Am*
L. *Southwest*
M. *TWA*
N. *United*
O. *USAir*
P. *Virgin Atlantic*
Q. *Western*

Inside SkyLav

If you've never navigated your way to that great rest spot in the sky — beware! Airplane lavatories are roughly the size of Kitty's litter box, and require the agility of Houdini and the muscle control of Jane Fonda before you can do anything in them.

Don't despair. Here's how to be a potty pro:

Ladies

Tip #1   Never wear pants you had to lie down in, hold your breath, and wriggle to zip up.

Tip #2   Never wear a jumpsuit unless it's factory equipped with a drop-seat.

Tip #3   Always check the toilet paper supply first — there'll be no good neighbor to hand you some under the stall.

Tip #4   Never confuse the "flight attendant" button with the "flush" button, if you value your privacy.

 Gentlemen

Tip #1 Aim, damn it . . . Aim!

Guaranteed:
All events witnessed
by flight attendants.

On entering the plane, a woman asks if she has a window seat. When told yes, she replies, "I can't sit there! I've just had my hair done."

A flight attendant tells new parents their baby seat will have to be placed in the overhead bin. Upon returning, she sees the baby seat has been obediently stowed — with the baby still in it.

A flight attendant observes a man trying to order another drink by talking directly into the overhead PA system, like the drive-thru at Jack-In-The-Box.

A businessman tries to board with an oversized carry-on bag. Since the plane is full, the flight attendant asks him to check it. Indignant, the man thunders, "Lady, do you know who I am?" The flight attendant immediately turns to the plane-load of passengers and says, "Excuse me, ladies and gentlemen. This man has forgotten who he is. Does anyone know him?"

A flight attendant is seen crawling around on her hands and knees, obviously looking for something. When asked what she's looking for, without missing a beat, she replies, "I'm looking for the glamour they promised me with this job."

Top Conversation Stoppers

**When you don't want to talk with the
person who'll be closest to you for
the next four hours.**

✈ "Whooh! I never shoulda had all those airport chili dogs."

✈ *"Zip-feh neggle-boo flok?"*

✈ "By the time we land, I'll have explained to you all the differences between whole and term life insurance."

✈ "Wanna see my rash?"

✈ "I have proof that our elected leaders are actually Nexus warriors from Alpha Centauri."

✈ "Have you heard about the great franchise opportunities in worm farming?"

✈ "Where I come from, even the sacred goats do not eat this good."

✈ "Can you get me that little . . . bag . . . in . . . . front . . . . . of . . . . . . you?"

Someone lay a good one on you? Tried a new one that worked like a charm? Send 'em in — see page 156!

The International Child Shusher

Is some little monster screaming, running around or kicking the back of your seat? If you've tried every polite gesture — from throat-clearing to intense glaring — now's the time to flip the card to the parents. If that doesn't work, hold up the next two pages and see which one does!

CURB YOUR YOUR KID!

P·l·e·a·s·e

Halten Sie bitte Ihr Kind zurück!

¡Frene su niño, por favor!

Réprimez votre enfant, s'il vous plaît!

Trattenga il Suo bambino, per favore!

The Top Things That Make You Crabby.

Just as you settle down in your seat to enjoy the flight, someone invariably does something to spoil the atmosphere. Here are the top passenger peeves from a recent survey. If yours are missing, see page 156.

- ✈ Snoring seatmates on your right.
- ✈ **Drunken seatmates on your left.**
- ✈ Seat-back recliners in front of you.
- ✈ **Screaming babies behind you.**
- ✈ Frequent lavatory-goers.
- ✈ **Beverage service carts blocking the aisles.**
- ✈ Hyperactive kids...with passive parents.
- ✈ **Hairsprayers who miss.**
- ✈ Little old ladies with big knitting needles.
- ✈ **Gabbers, while you're trying to watch the movie.**
- ✈ Gabbers, while you're trying to sleep.
- ✈ **Sleepers, when you're trying to gab.**
- ✈ Ignorant know-it-alls.
- ✈ **Armrest hoggers.**
- ✈ Cheap cologne from ten rows back.
- ✈ **Overpowering BO right next to you.**
- ✈ Overhead bin storage hogs.
- ✈ **Middle-seat diaper-changers.**

If You're Mad As Heck . . .

Passengers rarely know their rights when they feel they've been wronged. And Uncle Sam usually doesn't get involved in consumer disputes that go beyond lost luggage, overbooking and delays or cancellations on domestic flights — which are covered by specific rules. Beyond that, it's up to the airline.

For you, it comes down to two basic things: 1) Speak up. 2) Negotiate.

Airline customer service reps can usually answer your questions about their compensation policies. Also, refer to the fine print on your ticket. If you can read legalese, request a copy of the *Conditions of Carriage.*

Try to take care of any problem immediately. Speak up pleasantly and clearly to the airline's representative — or that person's supervisor. If you don't know the airline's policy, negotiate firmly for what you feel is a reasonable adjustment.

If that doesn't work, take notes and take names. Then take it up with the consumer relations

...You Don't Have To Take It Anymore.

department at the airline's headquarters. Get your travel agent involved. Or, if the situation is covered by government regulations, contact Uncle Sam for help.

Consumer issues

For information or action about lost or damaged baggage, overbooking, delayed or cancelled flights or other consumer issues regarding a U.S. or foreign airline, the Department of Transportation's Consumer Affairs Division can advise you of your rights under federal law and act as mediator with the airline.

Call: (202) 366-2220
M–F • 8:15 a.m.–4:45 p.m. ET

To put your complaint in writing, include your name, address, daytime phone number and a photocopy of your airline ticket, if possible. Be clear, to the point, and keep a copy of your letter.

Write: USDOT Consumer Affairs, I-25,
400 7th St., SW, Washington, D.C. 20590

Safety Issues

For action on complaints involving carry-on bags, airport security, child safety seats, hazardous materials, malfunctioning aircraft equipment or air-traffic procedures, the Federal Aviation Administration will investigate and report its findings to you.

Call toll free: 1-800-FAA-SURE
M-F • 8 a.m. - 4 p.m. ET
(202) 426-9365 in Washington, D.C.

To inquire about safety issues or to receive descriptive brochures — including the *FAA Guide To Publications* — write to:

FAA Public Inquiry Center
APA-200
Washington, D.C. 20591

More consumer information

➤ Contact the American Society of Travel Agents, who may help mediate your complaint against a travel agency, airline, hotel or travel supplier. Write to: ASTA Consumer Affairs, 1101 King Street, Alexandria, VA 22314 or call (703) 739-2782.

➤ Call your local Better Business Bureau. And check the state government listings in your phone book for any special offices dedicated to consumer affairs and resolving complaints.

➤ Contact your local TV, radio or newspaper's consumer action reporter with your story.

➤ For more detailed information on your rights, send $2 to the Aviation Consumer Action Project, a non-profit consumer group founded by Ralph Nader in 1971, for their brochure, *Facts & Advice for Airline Passengers*. Write: ACAP, P.O. Box 19029, Washington, D.C. 20036.

➤ The U.S. Consumer Information Center offers informative, low-cost brochures on travel, such as *Fly Rights* and *Your Trip Abroad*. Write for their free Consumer Information Catalog: P.O. Box 100, Pueblo, CO 81002.

Suggestion Box

Got a minute? Send us the time-savers, cost-cutters and in-flight insights we missed. Make note of the funniest *Incredible-But-True* comments you overhear — and before you forget — the *Things That Make You Crabby* on board.

Include your name and address if you dare. If we print your ideas in a future edition, you'll get an acknowledgement and a free book. Thanks!

Send it all to: CorkScrew Press, 4470-107 Sunset Blvd., Suite 234, Los Angeles, CA 90027

People I Know Who Oughta Have This Book*

_____

_____

_____

_____

_____

_____

_____

*weddings, promotions, birthdays, vacations,
honeymoons, did-me-a-favor, meetings,
conventions, brown-nose opportunities,
college-bound kids, reunions, phobias.

Laugh & Learn...

☐ **YES!** Send me more fun, practical books like *How To Fly!*

Name _____
Please Print Clearly

Address _____

City/State/Zip _____

How many of each would you like?

____ *EATING IN* $8.95   ____ *"It Was On Fire ..."* $8.95

____ *Crabby Book* $6.95   ____ *How To Fly* $5.95

Total cost of books $ _____

MI addresses add 4%   _____

Regular shipping*   _____

Rush shipping**   _____

TOTAL (U.S. funds) $ _____

Regular Shipping*
1 book . . . add $3.50
2-up . . . $1 per book
2-Day Rush Shipping**
1 book . . . add $6
2-up . . . $1 per book

☐ Check/money order — payable to PDS. *Do not send cash.*

☐ Please charge my ☐ VISA ☐ MasterCard

Card number_____Exp. date_____

Signature _____
Required for credit card orders

Mail to: PDS, 6893 Sullivan Road, Grawn, MI 49637
Or call **1-800-345-0096**. Please allow 2–4 weeks for delivery, or use rush service. Thank you for your order.

[HTF-01]

...When You Get Home!

Fun, affordable gifts from the publisher of *How To Fly*.

Happy Landing!
Thanks for flying with us.